Transfiguration

Patrice Merkouris

BookLeaf Publishing

Presentation by *BookLeaf Publishing*

Web: www.bookleafpub.com

E-mail: info@bookleafpub.com

ISBN: 9789395950701

First edition 2022

*To all the readers. You keep these pages
alive.*

I. ANGELS HITCHHIKE
ON HIGHWAYS

I stopped for one. A young man with black eyes.
Lost on the hacksawed interstate cutting through
Nowhere, Nevada. He was sorry
about the smell of burning pine.
"It's the climate," he said.
I told him it was fine, though the radio
whispered hymns to hurt him and the tyres
rumbled away
like distant thunder. So he ruffled the remains
of his battered wings and settled deep
into a world he could not see
from the passenger's seat. He had the patience of
someone waiting for questions. Meeting an
angel had me salivating
for some of that salvation he swallowed
and spat. So I asked how it felt to fall.
He only smiled,
"God told me you would say that."

II. WE STOPPED BY THE COAST

This place is my body.
— you're the stuff of dreams.
Which is?
— raw glass.

III. CALLING HOME FROM A PAYPHONE

I'm not asking for forgiveness just yet / I'm not even asking / for permission / I thought I'd be okay with / my body / for what it is / I'm not / here / I am / distilled to the worst of me / the inarticulate violence of a wound/ed animal / growing pain and grief / desire / unspeakable need / the emptiness You once / defined me / by antithesis /abandoned / in a land of middle ground.

IV. HE ASKED ME A QUESTION

Do not talk to me about honesty. Do not lie
to me about God. I'm only here because
I had the nerve to wake. The day stirring
in its own filth burns itself clean
out of our eyes. It's a reminder
to survive until given permission
to die. Live through the cruelty of summer.
The swelter and long hours of exposure.
An interrogation room
where that heat lamp we call the sun
sweats its answers
out of us.

V. THE MESA INN

5

Night unwinds for the push of dawn. The
breaking point—
a highway motel I do not remember
the trucks or the drivers or their baseball caps or
vests lined with wool for the winter even when
summer is yet to hold its breath.
I do not remember America. But here you are
haloed by savage gas station light. Sweat
running down the storm drain gutter of your
neck. That's gotta count for something.

VI. PLEASURE HUNTER

He asks, "what are you filling your heart with?"
Vicodin. Orange Juice. You—can spend the
night unravelling. I do it pretty well.
But I don't know how to speak
without begging for something. The words
falling apart in my mouth
like tender meat. I realise there are too many
ways to kill a man. I only know a few.
But we are drenched beneath the skin
tonight, the heat of you familiar
as yesterday's sun. You erode me with every
devout mouthful until I'm sick with wanting
what I do not need.

VII. GOD SPOKE TO ME IN FITFUL SLEEP

That night in my dreams he was made of water /
God poured a glass / swallowed him whole / told
me to tie him up / clip his wings / do anything /
God / dry-mouthed as a Hell dweller / thirsty as
the Devil himself / pleaded me to bring my
darkness down / on a thing of light.

VIII. BE NOT AFRAID

Invoking your name to test your patience.
Endure my company a little while longer. Tell
me about your childhood. Were you happy?
Did the voice of God sing you to sleep?

IX. I TELL HIM DIVINITY IS AN INFECTION

Your Father's name is an ulcer. It is a pest
in the ceiling, silent when it knows
I am listening. You are no longer holy
but your hands are still your hands
even if they won't touch me.

Come on, we've got sacrifices to make. I will ask
you once not to scream.

X. WE CYNICAL PROPHETS

Sitting on the platform with the rest, awaiting an answer to a question I never asked. The atheists smiling to hide the tightness in their jaws. The theists flexing their stigmatised wrists. A train hurtles by us. We mistake the sound for hooves, for trumpets, for something beautiful. I thought I heard you knocking.

XI. TWO SUNS RISE

My method of coercion splits
the sun in two. These days run
in reverse to bring us here, unscathed.
It's Thursday again and the sheets are clean.
He closed his eyes to the afternoon but the light
cuts us down the middle, that chasm of day
alive but fast fading. In the headlights
of an oncoming car I am untouchable.
Incandescent. Anointing whatever I can
get my hands on. Confusing the sun
with her pursuer. Do you see now
how we've learned to make saints
of delusional women? Canonised like a gun
in the mouth. Not that there's a difference
in the thick of it. The pseudo-silence
of a kiss. That labyrinth of memory
and its various twists of fate: to be known
and unknown, to be lost and found, to sleep
and wake, and sleep again.

XII. PHANTOM LIMB

I never had the guts to imagine us here.
On IV Saturdays, under sterile light,
you're a dying star. We'll both walk away
With holes burned into us.

Remember when you said
you owed me heaven but I didn't
have the stomach to take it?
I now know what you meant.

XIII. SOUTHWEST

I ran / my fingers down the notches of your
spine / clicked your joints into place to tell a
story of someone / holding himself together /
with threads of sinew and freckled flesh / pink
from the Texas sunlight / Southwest promised
land where you felt / ten pounds lighter / as your
feet met the overgrown earth / I wondered if I
could reach / my hand across the map / If you'd
crumble / or shatter.

XIV. I TREAT HIM LIKE THE MOON

Wearing the sun as a second skin.
We catch each other's eyes
through the window again, in the silence,
he answers every question in spite
of never having lived.
These thoughts of mine holding him
hostage between my ribs. Still I refuse
to regret any of it.

XV. YOU LIKE THIS

Excuse my hands while they find
something to do. The gallows will leave you
mostly as they found you, downtrodden,
break-neck, happy-go-lucky poor bastard you
were making it painfully easy
to love you. I see your martyr's smile
in every devastating stranger. In the light
 dividing itself to reach me.
I pray into your voicemail.
It doesn't mean anything.

XVI. FREEWAY

Six-lanes from Lexington to Indianapolis.
The dead of winter, black ice, wine-drunk;
bruises like a memory, resurfaced.
Hands on the mattress. My kiss
confusing the blood in his mouth. He eats my
confession while the store bought sponge cake
sweats its blackberry fever out on a knife.
The road keeps on unspooling but I'm
too starry eyed to drive.

XVII. A POPPY FIELD

Strange, that the first thing
the earth thought to give in
the wake of death was a sedative.
Do you ever think
we could be forgiven if we asked for it?
Or would the clamor of voices be
too much
like an explosion, and the sky
would cringe in memory?
I don't know. All I can recall is
the day rain became shrapnel
pounding its fists on the tin roof.
And we were drunk,
jumping the church fence, God,
I hated you.
I should have wrung your neck.
But it was love
and where did that leave us?
Searching the ground for poppies.

XVIII. ANOTHER PLACE

The throat of a corridor, a nod
in your direction not quite knowing how
to speak with an apparition, to be heard
over fungus thriving on shower tile.
The rancour of life and its passing footsteps
toward your foxhole, your grin, those eyes
like devil's water between my own
two hands holding open a door
for each bone I've unearthed
from the bedroom floor.

XIX. SO(U)LD

Like a bruise before it's healed, he tries
to free his hands from his body. Oh,
the things he'd do if he were only
his hands. Traverse the escape route
through touch alone. Know pain
but only vaguely. Those sharpened
shoulder blades once held wings.
Would you recognise yourself
without them? Once again a severed limb on
someone's autopsy table.
Inside of him, something
has lain dead for weeks. It's the metal
in his mouth. It's fear, he thinks.

XX. I HAVE NOT FORGIVEN EITHER OF US

Sunlight is bleeding through
the open window and he wants
to be baptised.
"You wanted me holy," he says. I deny
 for the third time: "If I wanted to play God I
would have torn the wings from your back like
baby teeth. Call it
growing pain. We're both better for it."
That's why you don't
blame me for the bruises. "It's biblical," I say,
"you're my Judas."
And I'm still punishing you for it. My hands
the hammers to nail you down.
With no intention of returning your pound
of flesh. Beg me harder
and I'll hit you again.

XXI. ANGELS SHOOT UP HEROIN IN PARKING LOTS

This story was not kind enough
to let us both live through it. I could tell you
about human teeth and the bite marks they leave
like syringes. But I'd rather you taste
the pillar of salt for yourself. I could be a liar
but who are you to give me the benefit
of the doubt. It's a thoughtless mercy for a girl
that is hands, a throat, a mouth. In a house built
on the killing floor. All my pillows
stuffed with feathers.